Prayer and the Common Life

Prayer and the Common Life

Thomas A. Langford

THE UPPER ROOM
Nashville, Tennessee

Prayer and the Common Life

Copyright © 1984 by the Upper Room. All rights reserved. No part of this book may be reproduced in any manner whatsoever without written permission of the publisher except in brief quotations embodied in critical articles or reviews. For information address The Upper Room, 1908 Grand Avenue, P.O. Box 189, Nashville, Tennessee 37202.

Unless otherwise identified, all scripture quotations are from the Revised Standard Version of the Bible (RSV) copyright 1946, 1952, and © 1971 by the Division of Christian Education, National Council of Churches of Christ in the United States of America, and are used by permission.

Scripture quotations designated Moffatt are from THE BIBLE: A NEW TRANSLATION by James Moffatt. Copyright, 1935 by Harper & Row, Publishers, Inc. By permission of the publishers.

Book Design: Harriette Bateman
Cover Design: John Robinson
First printing: March, 1984 (7)
Library of Congress Catalog Card Number: 83-51396
ISBN: 0-8358-0473-9
Printed in the United States of America

FOR
Ann Green,
Chris,
Colin,
children of love
and hope

Acknowledgments

Henry van Dyke: From "Joyful, Joyful, We Adore Thee." Reprinted with the permission of Charles Scribner's Sons from *The Poems of Henry van Dyke*. Copyright 1911, 1920 Charles Scribner's Sons; copyrights renewed.

William W. Reid: From "Give Thanks, My Soul." Reprinted with the permission of The Hymn Society of America.

G.A. Studdert-Kennedy: From *The Best of Studdert-Kennedy*. Published by Hodder & Stoughton Limited. Reprinted with the permission of the publisher.

Milton S. Littlefield: From "O Son of Man, Thou Madest Known" in *The Book of Hymns* published by the Board of Publications of The Methodist Church. Copyright © 1964, 1966. Reprinted with the permission of the publisher.

John Oxenham: From "Mid All the Traffic of the Ways." Reprinted with the permission of Desmond Dunkerly.

Thomas Merton: From *Spiritual Direction and Meditation*. Copyright © 1960 by The Order of St. Benedict, Inc. Published by The Liturgical Press, Collegeville, Minnesota. Used with permission.

Evelyn Underhill: From *An Anthology of the Love of God*. Reprinted with the permission of Tessa Sayle.

Edwin Markham: From "The Place Of Peace" published by *The Markham Review*. Reprinted with the permission of the Markham Archives.

Robert Frost: From "The Death of the Hired Man" from *The Poetry of Robert Frost* edited by Edward Connery Lathem. Copyright 1930, 1939, © 1969 by Holt, Rinehart and Winston. Copyright © 1958 by Robert Frost. Copyright © 1967 by Lesley Frost Ballantine. Reprinted by permission of Holt, Rinehart and Winston, Publishers, the Estate of Robert Frost, and Jonathan Cape Ltd.

Erik Routley: From "All Who Love & Serve Your City." Copyright © 1969 by Stainer & Bell. All rights reserved. Used by permission of Galaxy Music Corp., NY, and Stainer & Bell Ltd.

Frederick Herman Kaan: From "Sing We a Song of High Revolt." Copyright © 1968 by Galliard. All rights reserved. Used by permission of Galaxy Music Corp., NY, and Stainer & Bell Ltd.

Toyohiko Kagawa: From *Songs from the Slums*. Copyright renewal © 1963 by Lois J. Erickson. Used by permission of the publisher, Abingdon Press.

Catherine Cameron: From "God, Who Stretched the Spangled Heavens" published by Hope Publishing Company, 1967. Reprinted with the permission of the publisher.

Herbert O'Driscoll: From Hymn 170 in *The Hymn Book* published by the Anglican Church of Canada and the United Church of Canada. Used by permission of the author.

Carl Sandburg: From CORNHUSKERS by Carl Sandburg, copyright 1918 by Holt, Rinehart and Winston, Inc.; copyright 1946 by Carl Sandburg. Reprinted by permission of Harcourt Brace Jovanovich, Inc.

Contents

PREFACE 9
12/30 1. INTRODUCTION 11
1/6 2. BEGINNING THE DAY 16
1/13 3. DAILY WORK 22
1/20 4. AFTER WORK 30
1/27 5. STRESS 36
2/3 6. RECREATION 42
2/10 7. SYMBOLS 50
2/17 8. ALONE 57
2/24 9. FRIENDS 66
3/3 10. FAMILY 71
3/10 11. CHARITY 76
3/17 12. STYLE 83
3/24 13. CLOSE OF DAY 91

Preface

Christians often have an unsatisfied desire to pray. Yet we do not pray well and we live with a gnawing sense of inadequacy. We need to learn how to pray.

In a discussion among friends about prayer, one person concluded, "It's clear that we would all like to pray, but we just don't know how." In the face of such desperate assertion, is it possible to provide direction for a fulfilling prayer life? Can we learn to pray with meaning?

Prayer and the Common Life develops a practical model for prayer and suggests how prayer can be a part of our everyday experience. The following explorations are in two parts. An initial discussion examines characteristic times and experiences of each day and the opportunities they afford for prayer. Following the comments are discovery resources that can enrich awareness of the presence of God.

Making prayer a part of our daily life will renew our lives in God every day.

1. *Introduction*

In his early novel, *Under the Greenwood Tree*, Thomas Hardy describes the instrumental choirs in English churches a century ago. These volunteer musical groups played for a number of different village occasions and each member had to prepare a personal music book. Customarily, they copied their sacred music beginning at the front of the book and their secular reels, jigs, and hornblows moving from the back. A bizarre effect resulted when the tunes met and overlapped in the middle, Hardy writes.

Christians live in the overlap of the sacred and the secular. But what happens when the sacred and the secular meet? Sometimes the meeting is bizarre, a distortion of one reality by the other, or the distortion of both. Nevertheless, the story of these music books is the story of Christian life. We do not discover God apart from the usual events of ordinary life. God meets us in the events which make up our everydayness. Prayer does not lift us out of common life; it reinforces us for actual living.

> *Christians live where the sacred and the secular meet; the sacred and the secular meet in the Christian. Our daily rounds are the story of our spiritual lives.*

In the arena of overlap, in everyday events, are there guidelines for prayer? Can holy living occur in a secular setting? Some points of reference can be set, landmarks for guidance along the Christian way. Pointing to directing principles indicates possible paths towards meaningful prayer. These markers do not indicate necessary routes or inviolate rules that must be followed, but they may be helpful in finding your own ways of praying.

An ancient piece of spiritual guidance provides a first principle.

> Pray as you can pray,
> don't pray as you can't pray.

There are no stereotypes of prayer. Prayer for each of us is as varied as our different personalities, attitudes, and characters. While other peoples' prayer practices may serve as guides, no one else's form need be our own.

We must find natural ways of praying. What works for one person may not be helpful for another. We must explore our own ways—emphasis should be on *ways*—for in the rhythms of every life different times, changing sensibilities, and personal readinesses give rise to differing ways of being with God.

Life in the arena of overlap is complex. Desire for communion may come from experienced communion—a taste brings thirst—or it may arise from an excruciating sense of absence. Dryness of throat also creates intense thirst.

Our lives are not smooth. Ordinary life is a sequence of discovery and loss, of joy and sorrow, of meaning and the absence of meaning, of exhiliration and dogged determination. In human relationships we do not live at a single emotional pitch, and we do not always have the same sensitivity, even for those with whom we are most intimate. So it is with the divine-human relationship.

We experience God as present and as absent; as closer than breath and so distant as to be unfindable.

The Psalms are spiritual guides rich with honesty and a wide range of awareness. Listen to just a few exclamations.

Presence:

> I will sing of thy steadfast love,
>   O Lord, for ever;
> with my mouth I will proclaim
>   thy faithfulness to all generations.
> —Psalm 89:1

Absence:

> Why dost thou stand afar off,
>   O Lord?
> Why dost thou hide thyself in times
>   of trouble?
> —Psalm 10:1

Presence:

> My heart is steadfast, O God,
>   my heart is steadfast!
> I will sing and make melody!
> —Psalm 108:1

Absence:

> O Lord, my heart is not lifted up,
>   my eyes are not raised too high.
> —Psalm 131:1

The movement of life from affirmation to abject loss is a reality with which we all live. Prayer allows no pretensions, requires no artificial conditions. Presence and privation are both real. Sometimes one awareness is dominant, sometimes the other. Saints have known both of these circumstances. In sixteenth-century Spain lived two persons who both became saints in the Roman Catholic Church:

St. Teresa of Avila and St. John of the Cross. Both were remarkable Christians, both were exceptional spiritual guides. Yet these two persons seemed to find God in opposite ways. St. Teresa habitually gave thanks, praying joyfully in her awareness of the constant presence of God. St. John went through the debilitation of the "dark night of the soul," the seeming loss of the sense of the presence of God. Yet he prayed deeply even in his anguish.

Prayer opens one's own truth and depth to the depth and truth of God to establish through divine grace an authentic community of existence. Prayer is the interaction of being reached for and reaching for, of receiving and giving, of hearing and speaking, of sharing. And sometimes we experience renewal after privation. With George Herbert, the English poet, we say in surprise, "Who would have thought my shrivelled heart could have recovered greenness?"

Prayer begins where we are capable of beginning. God makes us capable of prayer. God calls us in our actual condition with our present sensitivities and capacities. God calls us as we live in the overlap of the sacred and the secular. Prayer, as creative communion, enhances our awareness of God and our ability and willingness to respond. Growth in community is a gracious work of God. God speaks to us as we are, utilizing our present to create a new future.

Prayer finds its lodging in everyday experience; our ordinary life is the setting for communion with God.

The arena of overlap does not allow us to control our situation. We cannot memorize rules that govern the way God comes to us, because God comes from many different directions and in many guises. In the face of the unexpected, we can only be ready and responsive. Further, we cannot learn by heart the way God's spirit will lead. We can only be faithful in obedience. Preparation to receive and to follow is the intention of spiritual discipline.

Protestant spirituality desperately needs prayer models that place lively communion with God into the overlap of the secular and the sacred arenas of everyday living. This book is an effort toward developing a useful model of how to live in the world and nourish our relationship with God.

After the discussion of each particular moment of everyday life that provides opportunity for prayer, you will find some suggestions and resources for using these moments of prayer. This section of each chapter is called "Discovery." Read, meditate upon, and use these materials for your discovery of God's presence.

2. Beginning the Day

> Prayer is as the pitcher that fetcheth water from the brook, therewith to water the herbs: break the pitcher and it will fetch no water, and for want of water the garden withers.
>
> —John Bunyan*

To wake up is to come consciously into the world. The world is there with its firmness and the rhythm of its change. God sets the night and the day, times of rest and times of activity. Changes of time establish frames for our relaxation and alertness. To awake is to awake to God's world, and it is an opportunity to come consciously, once again, into the presence of God.

The way in which awakening occurs varies as much as human beings. Some people awake instantly; when their eyes open they are as fully awake as they are at midday. Others simply stagger until the first cup of coffee or the last child has gone to school. These are not matters of good or bad; they are simply differences. Most of us know these differences. Because opposites attract, some marriages unequally yoke quick-risers with the slow-risers. (What one person may consider a harbinger of God's grace by happily saying "Good morning!" the other may per-

---

*John Bunyan, *Selections from the Writings of John Bunyan*, ed. Thomas S. Kepler (Nashville: The Upper Room, 1951), p. 13.

ceive as demonic noise.) What we do first, even in prayer, may be governed by what we are capable of doing first. Remember: Pray as you can pray, don't pray as you can't pray.

As we return to consciousness, we return to our awareness of being alive. We are conscious of our selves and our context; our interests set the horizons of our awareness. The external world possesses its own reality, but as we fix our vision we create—even insubstantially—the world in which we intend to live.

Our vision is finite—that is necessarily so—but we, by our attention, further limit the arena in which we live. The objective world presents its limitless expanse for our response, but our attention is restricted only to that part which is of interest to us: the room in which we awake, the person we first see, news, bath, and breakfast. Our awareness may not extend beyond our office, school room, the streets we travel, or the particular persons we meet.

The coming of a new day is not a gift for everyone. Many people experience evening exultation and morning tremors. A new day promises unwanted responsibility and unhappy encounters. Better to sleep than face unavoidable difficulties is a too-frequent attitude. It is an act of courage for many men and women to get out of bed, dress, and walk into the new day. To awake alone or to face an unfriendly day is a tragic but persistent human reality. To move into a new day requires faith and hope.

> *As we awake, we set—in a remarkable way—the horizons of our awareness. These horizons may be as small as the half-moons on our fingernails or as large as God. In our awakening we establish our world, the world in which we intend to live, the world of our attention, affection, and action. <u>As we come back to consciousness, we should also come to an awareness of God.</u>*

In our awakening we set horizons. Life is seen in large perspective or it is confined to closely restricted limits. The range of our awareness as we awake sets the range of our conscious world. This is why it is essential to begin our day with God. The spiritual principle is: seize the day!

> Seize this day for God!
> To begin the day with God is:
> to open our attention to the farthest horizons;
> to begin the day with a conscious sensitivity to the extending dimensions of life;
> to achieve a revolution,
> to place God at the center and ourselves on the periphery of attention;
> to have our imagination sweep across the earth,
> to become part of the human family, to be sensitive to earth sounds, to human hurt and hope;
> to begin the day responding to the most basic relationship, the relationship which properly puts into place every other relationship;
> to awaken to life with its richest potential.

It is not necessary to take someone else's mode of first prayer as a prescription of what you must do. Your world and relationships may take shape quickly or slowly. But in whatever way is natural, begin your day receiving the,

> Brightness of God, that breaks our night
> and fills the darkened soul with light...
> —Philipp Nicolai

Discovery

In *invocation* we seek God's presence.

> Come O Lord, like morning sunlight,
> Making all life new and free;
> For the daily task and challenge
> May we rise renewed in Thee.
> Come, O Lord, like ocean floodtides,
> Flowing inland from the sea;
> As the waters fill the shallows,
> May our souls be filled with Thee.
> —Milton S. Littlefield

In *adoration* we offer our prayer.

> Be thou my Vision, O Lord of my heart;
> Naught be all else to me, save that thou art—
> Thou my best thought by day or by night,
> Waking or sleeping, thy presence my light.
> —Ancient Irish

> Joyful, joyful, we adore Thee,
> God of glory, Lord of love;
> Hearts unfold like flow'rs before Thee,
> Opening to the sun above.
> Melt the clouds of sin and sadness;
> Drive the dark of doubt away;
> Giver of immortal gladness,
> Fill us with the light of day!
> —Henry van Dyke

In *affirmation* we recount God's gracious presence.

> New every morning is thy love
> Our wakening and uprising prove;
> Through sleep and darkness safely brought,
> Restored to life and power and thought.
> —John Keble

In *exaltation* we embrace the day with God.

> Praise God, from whom all blessings flow;
> Praise him, all creatures here below;
> Praise him above, ye heavenly host;
> Praise Father, Son, and Holy Ghost.
> —Thomas Ken

Verses of scripture may also be used. For instance,

> The eternal God is your dwelling place,
> and underneath are the everlasting arms.
> —Deuteronomy 33:27

> This is the day which the Lord has made;
> let us rejoice and be glad in it.
> —Psalm 118:24

Or other prayers may be useful, such as these that I have written:

> Give to me, O Lord, this day:
> A will to desire thee,
> A heart to love thee,
> A mind to seek thee,
> Strength to serve thee.
> Amen.

May this day begin, continue, and end with thee.
May the prayers begun this morning
be continued through the day.
Amen.

> O God,
> Order the beginning of this day.
> Guide our progress, and
> make our ending complete
> in thee. Amen.

Morning

O Lord God,
  Creator of all things,
    make us alive today to your creative spirit.
  Give us a sense of your presence.

We begin this day with adoration and thanksgiving.
  We are your creatures,
    you have created us for relationship with your
    self and we rejoice in this communion.

Prepare us for the events of this day.
  May we enjoy pleasure,
    be strong in adversity,
    faithful in love,
    sensitive to need,
    a sharer of grace.

Direct the activity and relationships of this day.
  May your Spirit find expression in all of
  our activities.

This is your day,
  and through this day we shall worship you.

  In the spirit and name of Jesus. Amen.

3. Daily Work

Bless us this day,
As we go to the work
You have given us to do. Amen.

Work helps identify who we are and gives importance to our existence. Work, ideally and in some cases actually, is a creative expression of the human spirit. Co-creators with God, we are sometimes given the possibility of making objects which are beautiful, useful, or good. Work sometimes provides significant vocation.

But not everyone is so fortunate. Some people are lost in impersonal processes and have little sense of achievement. Jobs may be drudgery. Some years ago as a guest preacher, I was eating in a home after morning worship. I asked my host what he did. He replied, "I work in a furniture plant." I asked what he did in the plant. "I sand pieces of wood about eighteen inches long." "Wood for what types of furniture?" I asked. "I don't know," was his answer.

Daily work may represent many things. It may impart satisfaction in itself. Work may be a means to other ends: as a way of supporting the family or of providing the goods of life. In the first case one goes to work to do the work; in the second place one goes to work to get the time over and receive the remuneration to use for one's own ends.

Within the range of possibility, it is still necessary to

wrest what significance we can from our daily work, to express our relation to God through our work.

Some moral axioms seem to apply:

The end result of our work should be constructive in society.
The activity should be lawful.
We should be able to work with the process and colleagues with integrity.
The sense of personal value and of contribution to others should be positive.

These ends may be gained from manual labor, artistic activity, person-related jobs, homemaking, provision of services, assembly line skills, selling, organizational administration, ministry. No stereotypes limit what sort of daily work may have significance. Unfortunately, people often do not discover the potential value in their work.

Enhancing work with significance is a Christian possibility. Daily work may be a service given to God; it may represent our part in the larger divine ecology; it may express a stewardship of physical strength, intellectual ability, and human relationships that have distinctive quality.

We express who we are in our daily work. Perhaps no other part of our activity reveals our basic temperament, our fundamental way of relating to others, or our ability to possess a sense of significance.

Basic values are given concrete embodiment in our going to our job, in our attitudes exhibited through our duties, and in the spirit with which we work.

A young, successful businessman in Canada once said to me: "It is not possible to employ Christian principles in the business world." If it is not, then the world is not God's world. But it is true that the world also is infected with evil, and business practice may be carried on with dishonesty or indifference to human values, or simply for selfish gain. It is precisely in such areas of secular life that Christian character must be revealed.

The spirit with which we do our daily work may express the presence of the Holy Spirit in our lives. In the book of Ecclesiasticus (in the Apocrypha) there is an arresting statement about wise and devout people, people who do not hold eminent positions, but who "maintain the fabric of the world." The text is not wholly clear, but an acceptable translation is, "Their daily work is their prayer" (Ecclus. 38:34). The comment is suggestive for the Christian, as our given tasks may be an opportunity for worshipful service.

Brother Lawrence practiced the presence of God in the kitchen of his monastery. In *The Practice of the Presence of God* he writes, "So, likewise, in his business in the kitchen (to which he had naturally a great aversion), having accustomed himself to do everything there for the love of God, and with prayer, upon all occasions, for his grace to do his work well, he had found everything easy, during the fifteen years he had been employed there."

Pray for the daily task as you do the daily task.

Dr. Erdman Palmore, who does research on human aging at Duke University, says that the one correlation which seems to stand is that meaningful work tends to go with longer life; to be happily engaged in daily work actually adds years to one's life.* Because daily work is so significant, it is important that we find vocational responsibility that is challenging, creative, and fulfilling. And for

---

*Charles Braswell, *Issues in Education*, Radio Broadcast, September 13, 1981.

the Christian, going to work with God underwrites the importance and the possibility of our daily tasks.

Work may be an activity done with God. Business activity, keeping a home, the practice of law or medicine, manual labor, selling, or any activity can be done with God. This is not a pretentious spirituality. Quietly and faithfully we work with God. The people we meet become an opportunity for intercession. The people we serve become an opportunity for expression of Christian grace.

Work becomes an opportunity for our being co-creators with God. Isn't it the case that we often feel closest to another person when we do something together, such as listening to music, working side by side, eating, playing? So it may be that as we engage in activities with God, we feel the reality of divine-human companionship.

William Law comments in *A Serious Call to a Devout and Holy Life*, "It is therefore absolutely necessary for all Christians, whether men or women, to consider themselves as persons that are devoted to holiness, and so order their common ways of life, by such rules of reason and piety, as may turn it into continual service unto Almighty God."

Honest work is work done well, work done as unto God. It is a good feeling to come in tired from work well done. Passively to accept mediocrity is to be unfaithful. Being freed by God from the necessity to prove ourselves by our work, we are freed to do our work as good craftsmen, as honest workers, as farmers, as truckers, as employers, as workers in media, and servants of justice and human need.

Our intensity about our work should not, however, be so controlling that we do not relax and accept the unexpected interruption. Interruptions may be special opportunities. The intrusion of the unexpected may give rise to ways of being gracious. Nothing is too petty to provide opportunity for significant reaction. At times, interruptions are necessary to break us out of our dominant preoccupation and make us responsive to human need. What we do as a primary task should not make us unavailable for others in special need.

Who knows around what corner you will meet Jesus focused in human need? Who knows ahead of time which glance, word, or touch will convey a call to special discipline? We must be open and ready for these encounters. It is disconcerting but also embracing to face the continual possibility of meeting God.

But do not look only for the exceptional. For it is principally in the ordinary, in the usual tasks, that we meet God and it is in doing these tasks that we most clearly reveal our relationship with God.

> *Work is given by God and may be done with a sense of God's participating presence.*

Discovery

We may assist our sense of the importance of work as we set the activity into right perspective. For instance, we may pray.

> Dear Lord,
>   may the business of this day
>   be given purpose,
>   and depth,
>   and vitality,
>   by your Holy Spirit.

We may find the use of some hymns helpful.

> Work shall be prayer, if all be wrought.
>   As thou wouldst have it done;
> And prayer, by thee inspired and taught,
>   Itself with work be one.
> —John Ellerton

> Forth in thy name, O Lord, I go,
> My daily labor to pursue;
> Thee, only thee, resolved to know
> In all I think or speak to do.
>
> The task thy wisdom hath assigned,
> O let me cheerfully fulfill;
> In all my works thy presence find,
> And prove thy good and perfect will.
> —Charles Wesley

> O Thou who dost the vision send
> And givest each his task,
> And with the task sufficient strength:
> Show us Thy will, we ask;

> Give us a conscience bold and good;
> Give us a purpose true,
> That it may be our highest joy,
> Our Father's work to do.
> —Jay T. Stocking

One-word prayers. Choose a word for a day, such as *peace* or *justice* or *patience* or *bread*. Through the day utter this one word to God. Allow your imagination to move across family, the world, people and places of special concern. Use it as you meet different situations. Make it the focal point of your sensitivity for this day.

> Give thanks, my soul, for labours,
> that strength and days employ;
> but know the Master's purpose
> brings toil as well as joy.
> —William W. Reid

O Son of Man, Thou madest known,
Through quiet work in shop and home,
The sacredness of common things,
The chance of life that each day brings.

O Workman true, may we fulfill
In daily life Thy Father's will;
In duty's call, Thy call we hear
To fuller life, through work sincere.
—Milton S. Littlefield

> Because this is my Work, O Lord,
>   It must be Thine,
> Because it is a human task
>   It is divine.
> —G. A. Studdert-Kennedy

Work

O Lord, you have given us the privilege of work.
  Help us to work in a spirit and with a care that is worthy of a disciple of yours.

May we do our work well.
  Whatever the task, help us to give it our best thought and effort.

May we relate in Christian love to those with whom we work, to those whom we meet and those to whom we talk. Give significance to our encounters.

May we find joy in the concrete activity of our work.

May we begin and continue our work with a sense of your presence. Help us to share, in appropriate ways, your presence with others.

When the work time is over, may we have a sense of faithful service done, for good fulfilled, and of a day spent with you.

In the spirit of the Carpenter, our Lord. Amen.

4. After Work

Work constitutes a good part of our time. But as only a part it must be kept in proper perspective: work is important but not ultimate. It is significant but not the only activity of value. When time comes to leave the office or factory, the store or truck, it is time to set some activities aside and to be renewed by other relationships and activities.

Quitting Time. The close of work concludes one period of the day and begins another. As you put down your pencil, close your drawer, check out at the clock, put on your coat, lock the door or say good-bye—release the day's activities into God's keeping.

> Offer a final prayer for the work and a concluding intercession for co-workers.
> Offer thanksgiving for the end of one activity and the beginning of another part of the day.
> Move beyond the daily work with a prayer for the next events: family, meal, avocational activity, time for other tasks and relaxation. Ask for God's refreshment from work faithfully done and for God's renewal for the rest of the day, its relationships and activities.

Those who have set work hours are fortunate. Definite breaks help to divide the day, allow for stopping and new beginning. Clear change helps to regulate life. Those who do not have sharp change—a housewife, a farmer, or a person with an office at home—must take initiative to set patterns for work and relaxation. Clear transition from one part of a day to another may renew physical, emotional, and spiritual strength.

We have learned from our culture that the day's work is set aside with a "happy hour," a time to unwind, renew joy, and affirm emancipation. Such an idea may make work too negative. Nevertheless, after work there should be a happy hour, a time of new contexts, family, and friends. We should recognize the rhythm in the day and sense that this part of the day promises newness.

Two movements are of value: 1) release the day's work and 2) look with fresh expectation to the next encounters.

To be able to release a day's work is significant—but difficult. Many of us are workaholics. We carry our work inside us and cannot release our anxiety. It is important to remember that work done for God must ultimately be left to God.

Let's take the transition in steps. Work concludes. For many there is a briefcase syndrome; all unfinished work is stuffed in to be taken home (not that it is usually done, but it salves the conscience to make the pretense). It also testifies to our inability to simply stop and commend the work of the day to God.

Amid unsolved problems and unresolved tensions, we need, by a discipline of decision, to "simply stop" and commit a passed time to God.

To be sure, there are times when work legitimately spills over the normal work time. There are periods when work must consume our energy. There should be good heart in meeting these times, but we should recognize when there is no such demand by our work and when we should set job responsibilities into more limited dimensions.

Each of us is different. For some, who have heavy

responsibilities, whose work is primarily thought, who have no special location in which they work, concluding work is especially difficult. For others, who work odd hours, switching shifts, the conclusion may also be strange or of their own invention. In the pattern of each life, there is a time of beginning and a time of stopping, and each usually needs to be clearly defined.

We need to work when we work; we need to stop work when we stop.

This is homely wisdom but has to do with a sense of God's sovereign rulership, with a release of guilt and undue ambition, and, most of all, with being present with the persons and tasks which are appropriate at a given time. Hence we move from one activity to another, we close out one time of the day and begin another.

Closure and openness constitute a transition which offers opportunity for penance and thanksgiving, for good grace of forgiveness and joy over the possibility of the future.

For many the most trying time of the day is commuting home. Commuting is for some a time of stupor, for others a time to vent aggressiveness and anger. The car, the train, or the bus become the arenas for evaluating our lives, expressing our hopes, and anticipating our future. Probably too many decisions are made in the context of aggravating traffic and frustrating stop lights.

Perhaps the time of commuting is the most unused and therefore most promising time for setting our lives in the context of God. Here the question of attention is crucial. If driving, one must be attentive to the traffic. But at the same time one can sing, quote, or simply relax into the keeping of God. A relaxed attentiveness is the needed sense in the closing crunch of the business day.

Commuting may be a time of communion. Travel provides a good time to release the past and anticipate the future.

This leads to the second moment: fresh expectation of the next events. We come home, or prepare for a meal, or are with friends or family, or take up a vocational interest, go to night classes, or move to recreation or service projects. Whatever the next occasions, they are also to be anticipated as gifts of God's goodness and as ways in which God can be loved and served.

Time away from work has the possibility of fulfilling our lives if it is purposefully given to God and seen as another arena of God's sovereign rulership.

Work for the day is over; new opportunities for significant meaning are waiting to be found.

Beyond work, the most obvious expressions of our style of life are in family, recreation, or works of charity. These we shall explore in succeeding chapters.

Discovery

> The Lord be with us as we walk
> Along our homeward road;
> In silent thought or friendly talk,
> Our hearts be near to God.
> —John Ellerton

> Come as the wind; sweep clean away
> What dead within us lies,
> And search and freshen all our souls
> With living energies.
> —Andrew Reed

Establish some routines. As you cross a particular bridge or street or city limit, set the work behind and look forward to home. As you get into your car, stop, look around, know that God is present. As you say good-bye make it a benediction. As you say hello make it a grace note.

> Praise the Lord!
> O give thanks to the Lord, for he is good;
> for his steadfast love endures for ever!
> —Psalm 106:1

After Work

Most gracious God,
  You have given activity and cessation of work,
    you have set different times and seasons for life.
  Help us to embrace each new opportunity with the
    confidence that you are always present with us.
  Help us to release our efforts into your keeping.
  For work and challenge,
    we thank you.
  For the change of time and new tasks,
    we thank you.
  For jobs and release from jobs,
    we thank you.
  For vocational and avocational opportunity,
    we thank you.
  For colleagues and family,
    we thank you.
  For the freedom to contribute to the well-being
      of others,
    we thank you.

  In the name of him who is ever with us,
    even Jesus Christ our Lord. Amen.

5. Stress

Days do not always fall into order. Some days confront us with bad news: out of work, emergencies, hostility, pain, exhaustion. Some days have no structure on which to fix meaning. Rather, we face questions of self-worth, challenge, impotence, and failed hope. Stress is a part of every person's life.

A young mother whose father had been in a coma for three months and who might continue in this condition indefinitely said in anguish, "Sometimes illness brings a family together. But my father's illness is tearing our family apart." Tensions carry a cost.

An unemployed black man in Chicago answered the question, "How do you feel about being laid off?" by replying, "I'm numb. I only want a chance to make a life for myself, my wife, and baby. But I can find no way." When the economy is unstable, people who never dreamed of the likelihood find themselves unemployed, underemployed, or wrongly employed.

Employers, employees, or fellow employees can ruin a day. Work can be distressful, relationships can be abrasive, and work may be done with an undercurrent of anger or resentment. A job can become bondage. "I struggle through work," a man said, "for the day to get over."

Family relations may also be stressful. "My marriage is destroying all of my life," a young woman said. Marital separation and divorce, parent and child estrangement, rivalry of sisters or brothers constitute some of the common casualties of modern life. These strains are not easily resolved. Attempting to do good, our actions turn out to be wrong; an intended touch becomes a searing scratch; a word provokes a war.

No one is immune to stress. To live in the arena of overlap is to feel the painful pull and push of harsh reality.

Sometimes our days lose order because we do not have enough discipline to give them structure. We allow daily events to control us and drive us mercilessly. The wave of happenings carries us along, and we do not order our days with a clear sense of what is most important. Sometimes our days lose structure because events we cannot control overwhelm us. We are helpless to do more than respond to that which is given and seek to survive.

Sometimes we attempt too much, sometimes too little—both pride and sloth may bring the ruin of possible achievement. But sometimes we are victims of capricious nature or human sin. Demonic structures impose upon us and bring depravation, hurt, and loss of a sense of personal meaning.

Any day may bring stress. Some stress is beneficial, but too much stress makes us vulnerable to illness, ruptured relationships, and emotional distress. Modern medicine has found cures for many traditional ills; modern life has increased the incidence of other, equally destructive forms of sickness—high blood pressure, tension headaches, heart trouble, ulcers.

Too much stress may also bring spiritual debilitation. All of life is tied together; our thinking, our feeling, our human and divine relationships are parts of one whole person. Changing one dimension brings change throughout the others. For good or bad, for health or illness, we are one person. Spiritual well-being is essential to wholeness of life. Our spiritual condition may affect the totality of our life, and the rest of our life may affect our spiritual well-being.

Spiritual health, especially in times of general distress, provides a gyroscope for living.

We must speak sensitively about these matters. Only one who has been in a particular distressing situation knows fully what a challenge to religious faith, to human relationships, and trust in God these experiences can be. One cannot speak smugly or patronizingly, but the person living through such a hard time must remember:

God is present. Along hard paths and lonely ways, through deep trouble and pain, God is present.

Faith becomes truly significant as life is faced in its most serious challenge. Regular structures of life help us meet the unexpected, but the course of life does not always follow regular routines. It is in these unordered and disordered times that stress is felt most keenly. In stressful situations, there are no easy answers. Casual or glib answers are unacceptable. Friends may stand by with prayerful and empathetic support, and this is critical; but in a situation of anxiety, immediate reliance upon God is essential. The American folk hymn reminds us, "There is a balm in Gilead, to make the wounded whole." And the psalmist has affirmed,

> God is our refuge and strength,
>   a very present help in trouble.
> Therefore we will not fear
>   though the earth should change,
>   though the mountains shake in the heart of the sea;
>   though its waters roar and foam,
>   though the mountains tremble with its tumult.
> —Psalm 46:1

Discovery

>Discouraged in the work of life,
>Disheartened by its load,
>Shamed by its failures or its fears,
>I sink beside the road;
>But let me only think of thee,
>And then new heart springs up in me.
>—Samuel Longfellow

My God, my God, why hast thou forsaken me?
  Why art thou so far from helping me?
. . . .
He has not despised or abhorred
  the affliction of the afflicted;
and he has not hid his face from him,
  but has heard, when he cried to him.
—Psalm 22:1, 24

>When the storms of life are raging,
> Stand by me;
>When the storms of life are raging,
> Stand by me;
>When the world is tossing me
> Like a ship upon the sea;
>Thou who rulest wind and water,
> Stand by me.
>—Charles A. Tindley

>'Mid all the traffic of the ways,
>Turmoils without, within,
>Make in my heart a quiet place,
>And come and dwell therein.
>—John Oxenham

>O Love that wilt not let me go,
>I rest my weary soul in thee;
>I give thee back the life I owe,
>That in thine ocean depths its flow
>May richer, fuller be.
>—George Matheson

From every stormy wind that blows,
From every swelling tide of woes,
There is a calm, a sure retreat:
'Tis found beneath the mercy seat.
—Hugh Stowell

Lead, kindly Light, amid th' encircling gloom,
Lead thou me on!

The night is dark, and I am far from home;
Lead thou me on!

Keep thou my feet; I do not ask to see
The distant scene; one step enough for me.
—John Henry Newman

My soul, be on thy guard;
Ten thousand foes arise;
The hosts of sin are pressing hard
To draw thee from the skies.

O watch and fight and pray;
The battle ne'er give o'er;
Renew it boldly every day,
And help divine implore.
—George Heath

Stress

O God,
There are times of great difficulty in our lives.
> We are hurt, alone, depressed, tense, and afraid. Our lives are out of joint, our world is oppressive, and we need your comforting presence.

> When life is hard, be with us.
> When there is no order, still sustain us.
> When we have no strength to reach out, continue to hold us.
> When we experience undue stress, touch us with thy relaxing grace.

Give us
> strength to endure,
> a will to trust you,
> a heart that is faithful.

But, most of all, we, in this time of trouble,
> trust:
>> your patience,
>> and love,
>> and presence,
>> and grace.

> Into your hands we commend our spirits. Amen.

6. Recreation

> We should certainly be serious in our search for
> God—nothing is more serious than that. But we
> ought not to be constantly observing our own
> efforts at progress and paying exaggerated attention
> to "our spiritual life!"
> —From *Spiritual Direction* by Thomas Merton

God is sovereign over our entire life, including free time and recreation. An important part of Christian character is an ability to laugh deeply, to be able to enjoy life thoroughly. Recreation can be re-creative.

To relax thoroughly is as much an expression of Christian goodness as is hard work. It is to enjoy the reign of God over the totality of our lives. Yet, many of us find it difficult to be relaxed about relaxation; we feel that we must work hard, be responsible, and be serious about life.

A friend and I were driving across campus. He asked where we were going for our vacation. After I told him, he said, "What work are you taking to do?" Spontaneously I told him what I hoped to get done while away. Then he laughed. "You are a perfect example of the Protestant work ethic. Have you ever really gone on a vacation just to relax?" The truth was that since I had been an adult I had not taken a vacation just to have a holiday. He forced me to face my attitude toward recreation. And I have come to understand that to take time off for enjoyment can be good in itself.

We often fail at our recreation because we do not relax.

A sense of guilt prevents relaxation. Not having done what we think we should have done prevents us from doing with a free heart what we are now doing. Isn't it often true that vacations can be the most vexing times for family relationships? How many nerves have been frayed by visiting "interesting" places? Car rides can be torment, and parents say to children, through clinched teeth, "Shut up, keep your hands off one another, and stay in your seat. You are going to have a good time if it kills you." How often after a holiday we come home to recuperate.

Life has rhythms. It moves between intensity and relaxation, between work and leisure. Both dimensions of life are enhanced by conscious sharing with God.

Recreation may legitimately be a time for renewal of strength to do one's regular work. For some, their chief fulfillment and their contribution can best be made through their vocation. For these persons, recreation may be a time of refreshment, a time of renewal of strength for the central work of life. But there are no stereotypes; one need neither be obsessed by work nor obsessed by not allowing work to be obsessive.

Grace brings good humor, for grace leads us to look at ourselves under God. We can take ourselves with a seriousness which is not final. Joy is God's gift. It adds reach and depth to life. Human life which reflects God's sovereignty or graciousness is laced with joy, as goodness is conveyed through happiness.

When free time is given, it is to be thankfully embraced. A thing worth doing is worth doing with joy.

For many Americans, leisure and work represent different aspects of their lives, and the resulting imperative is to find meaning in and for the whole of life. In this sense recreation is good in itself; it is not simply a time out in order to gain strength to work harder. To enjoy is to find true meaning, and to enjoy life can be also an enjoyment of God. But some people work too hard at recreation; play takes on the success intensity of work. <u>It is a special spiritual gift to be able to work hard and well and then to release that effort and relax into the enjoyment of sheer fun.</u>

> *Creation is renewed by recreation; re-creation prevents de-creation and brings forth new life.*

Recreation serves creativity, and creativity is the end of the human journey as well as its beginning.

In a work-oriented culture, recreation is often justified only in terms of making one more efficient in work. Hence, it is difficult to capture a positive sense of the value of recreation in and for itself. But we can find good in time away from ordinary work responsibility.

Recreation may be found in alternative activities, in avocational interests, through involvement in projects for which we have gifts or graces not utilized in our daily work. We may turn to creative activities which give vent to special talent, or we may explore opportunities for person-centered activity.

Many persons in our culture find it necessary to strike a balance of work and leisure, of intense effort and relaxation. And God, who is sovereign over all of life, graciously attends to the renewing moments, to the times of happiness, to the fun experiences of life.

> *It is a gracing of life to be able to laugh thoroughly, to move at a different pace, to embrace our existence as good.*

Recreation is as much a gift of God as good hard work or as a challenging task. Recreation sets life in a different frame of reference. It opens horizons in new directions, it lets winds blow in cross current, and puts persons in altered relations.

All this may be simply good in itself, needing no other justification.

All this may lead to special opportunity in avocational pursuits and provide a constructive complement in life.

All this may bring renewed vitality for the principal vocation of life. But whatever the mode, recreation is a gift of God.

Recreation is not a time which means freedom from God. It is freedom given by God and freedom in God.

Karl Barth, the Swiss theologian, has commented in *Church Dogmatics*, "A being is free only when it can determine and limit its activity... [God's] creative activity has its limit in the rest from His works determined by Himself, i.e. the rest of the seventh day."

So then, there remains a sabbath rest for the people of God; for whoever enters God's rest also ceases from his labors as God did from his.
—Hebrews 4:9

A leader of the church recently said, "I haven't taken a vacation in over twenty years. I don't need one." A friend commented, "He may not think that he needs a vacation, but a lot of other people do." We have no reason to take pride in not being able to relax, although the forms and manners of relaxation may vary greatly.

Relaxation is a manifestation of trust in God's kingly rule.

The word *holiday* comes from *holy day*, time set apart for religious observance. The source of the word stands as a reminder that holidays can be a time of grace when we stop usual activities and find joy and renewal in God.

Vacations do not mean leaving God out of our lives. Rather they are opportunities for making space for God, for joy, and for human renewal. The sabbath time reminds us that God also blesses rest as a valid part of life.

Recreation also witnesses a relaxation about our development in the spiritual life. Thomas Merton observes the following in *Spiritual Direction:*

> In trying to turn out too much work for God we may well end up by doing nothing for Him at all and losing our interior life at the same time. St. Therese of Lisieux wisely reminds us that "God has no need of our works: He has need of our love."

Brother Lawrence comments in *The Practice of the Presence of God* about a woman seeker, "She seems to me full of good will, but she would go faster than grace. One does not become holy all at once."

Recreation means relaxation, a release from the usual busyness and striving to do well and be successful. Relaxation comes as a relationship. Relaxation is God's gift as God's presence; relaxing into the undergirding arms of God provides a released sense about life.

Discovery

> Ten thousand thousand precious gifts
> My daily thanks employ;
> Nor is the least a cheerful heart
> That tastes those gifts with joy.
> —Joseph Addison

Think about your vacation.

A good vacation carries double value: release from usual contexts and relationships to a new arena. Choose a different environment or a new set of activities. Move into new rhythms for daily life, relax about time. Relax about people. Don't rush. Enjoy each person and moment. Make companionship with God central to the activities. Allow renewal to take place.

Think about your sports.

What do you truly enjoy, and what brings renewal? How much quality time should you give to this? Don't allow recreation to be an intensification of your usual activities. Give yourself to what you have chosen to do. Consciously allow the presence of God to become a central reality in your activity.

Think about the people you are with.

Recreation is not only renewal of one person, it is often a renewal of life together. Time off may become time for other people. How can free time be made significant to our relationships? Vacation is a special time to enjoy family and friends.

> They who wait for the Lord
>   shall renew their strength,
> they shall mount up with wings
>   like eagles,
> they shall run and not be weary,
>   they shall walk and not faint.
> —Isaiah 40:31

> Bless the Lord, O my soul;
> and all that is within me,
> bless his holy name!
> Bless the Lord, O my soul,
> and forget not all his benefits.
> —Psalm 103:1-2

> Lord, thou hast been our dwelling place
> in all generations.
> Before the mountains were brought forth,
> or ever thou hadst formed the earth
> and the world,
> from everlasting to everlasting
> thou art God.
> —Psalm 90:1-2

Make your recreation an offering to God. Enjoy the activity and being with friends. Use the different time for new awareness. Give some of your freedom to a quiet walk, the enjoyment of weather, a time to relax. Enlarge your awareness of nature and other people. Do what you do with a full heart.

Recreation

We thank you, O Lord, for the mercies of life,
   for hard work and relaxation.
   May we happily embrace every time given.
Renew our spirits, O Lord, in our times of fun,
   in recreation, in our time off.

All life is your gift:
   families and friends,
   the rhythms of life,
   pleasure, beauty,
   and the chance to enjoy them.

You are sovereign, O Lord.
   May every moment of our life be subject to your reign.
   Refresh us with your Holy Spirit.

   In Jesus' name. Amen.

7. Symbols

Ordinary events of the day may become the media of God's presence. Occurrences in the usual course of life may be reminders of the depth of life.

God leads us to spiritual truth through ordinary tokens of everyday experience.

Memories are evoked by sight, touch, hearing, or smells. Encounters which are a part of each day may mediate a profound sense of crucial moments. The physical senses often recall a person, place, or experience that was crucially important in our lives.

Ordering our day through concrete events is the most constructive way of relating the sacred and secular dimensions of living.

Francis de Sales, a sixteenth century Roman Catholic saint, indicates the importance of using every object, every event as a medium of approach to God. In *Introduction to the Devout Life* he writes,

So you see, Philothea, how we may extract good thoughts and holy aspirations from everything found amid the changes of this mortal life.... Blessed are they who turn creatures to the glory of their Creator and use their own vanity to honor the truth. Indeed, as St. Gregory Nazianzen says, "It is my custom to refer all things to my spiritual profit."

The power of association sparks memory and makes one experience convey the reality of another experience. An amusing occurrence reminds me of this fact. I was driving an elderly friend to her summer home. She asked if we could go by the post office. Then she said, "You know, the way I remember the combination to my post office box from summer to summer is by association. I remember the combination by recalling a story." When we arrived at the post office, she said, "Don't stop. I can't remember the story I use to remember my combination."

Memory may work that way, for we do associate one event with another and remember one event by another. Sometimes hearing a song reminds us of another particular time or person or place. Sometimes seeing a wedding ring recalls another person. Sometimes visiting a beach, looking at the surf, smelling the sea reminds us of a previous experience. Anything may revive memory of earlier occasions or persons.

> *Ordinary events may evoke a sense of sacred places and sacred times; usual encounters may transport us to pivotal moments of life.*

Thomas Hardy asks a question about sensitive awareness in his poem, "Awareness."

> When the Present has latched its postern behind
>   my tremulous stay,
>   And the May month flaps its glad green leaves
>   like wings,
> Delicate-filmed as new-spun silk, will the neighbors say,
>   "He was a man who used to notice such things"?

Special places also possess this power. A sanctuary is set apart to remind us of God. An outdoor worship setting may, simply by entering it, make us sensitive to God's presence. Observance of Sunday as a day of worship sets the context for seeing our time within the frame of God's presence and activity. And the loss of special places and times has negative consequences for the experience of meaning.

In practicing the presence of God, it is helpful to allow ordinary places and times to be so identified with special meaning that they become reminders of ultimate reality. The tokens may be small or the events of an everyday sort, but these may also be openings into deeply significant meaning. Like peepholes, which may be tiny, concrete symbols can allow one to see a whole panorama.

Tertullian, a second-century Christian, found that by attaching special significance to ordinary events he could be more consciously aware of God's presence. So when he washed his hands, he thought of God's cleansing. When he ate, he was thankful for God's bounty. Small events of the usual day become openings to the realization of God's presence.

What are possible tokens in our daily rounds? They may be almost anything.

There are usual ones—usual because so many people have found them helpful: grace before meals, regular worship on Sunday, prayer in the morning, prayer at the close of the day. Take only a couple of these as examples. Eating is among the most regular occurrences of our lives, and it is important to recognize God's presence in the act of eating. We pray with our Lord, "Give us this day our daily bread," and as we receive our bread, we take opportunity to give thanks. Regular grace before meals can become a graciously regulating moment of our day.

Regular worship in Christian community is fundamental in Christian life. Worship focuses life upon God. It is responsive affirmation to God's capturing love. Worship is the most distinctive posture of Christian life. It is not optional, for it expresses who we are at the most basic level of our lives. This is the chief event of structured

Christian living. Grace before meals and worship are among the usual tokens of daily prayer.

Unusual tokens can also help to order life in relation to God. These are unusual because we seldom use or think about them. But they may be usual in terms of our ordinary course of life. A few illustrations may be suggestive.

- A particular chair: a place one uses to sit and pray.
  So each time we sit in that chair there is an immediate sense of reverent expectation.
- A walk to the office or store or place of employment: a time to place the day in God's keeping,
  to pray for colleagues and work.
- Washing dishes: a time to relax into the presence of God and allow the washing of each glass or dish to become a prayer for someone.
- A coffee break: a regular time when one allows the coffee to become a sacrament of sharing.

A friend tells me that she owns a diesel car. It takes a minute for the ignition to warm up before the car will start. She makes this a time of prayer. The pattern is regular and is now a conditioned response. Each time she turns on the switch, she automatically falls into prayer. She orders her day as she starts her car.

A businessman makes his reference to his daily calendar serve as a reminder of intercessory prayer for the persons he is to meet and the particular business he is to transact. He connects his daily schedule with his neighbor love.

Cleaning the home, a vase, photos, and books may be occasions for prayer for the one called to mind. So also writing letters, planning a party, baking a cake or pie, or washing clothes. So also at work, one may have opportunity through concrete tokens for prayer, such as the reading of mail, personal encounters, decisions about money. Even saying hello or good-bye may be a moment of prayer.

Discovery

I come in the little things,
Saith the Lord:
Yea! on the glancing wings
Of eager birds, the softly pattering feet
Of furred and gentle beasts, I come to meet
Your hard and wayward heart.
—From *An Anthology of the Love of God*
  by Evelyn Underhill

Earth's crammed with heaven,
And every common bush afire with God;
But only he who sees, takes off his shoes,
The rest sit round it and pluck blackberries,
And daub their natural faces unaware
More and more from the first similitude.
—From *Aurora Leigh*
  by Elizabeth Barrett Browning

> God be in my head,
> And in my understanding;
>
> God be in mine eyes,
> And in my looking;
>
> God be in my mouth,
> And in my speaking;
>
> God be in my heart,
> And in my thinking;
>
> God be at my end,
> And at my departing.
> —*Sarum Primer*

Select a specific place for prayer. One or two simple symbols may remind you that this is a special place and as you stand, sit, or kneel you know that you are in the presence of God. For instance, this may be a chair. On the table beside the chair place a Bible or small cross, a devotional guide or hymn book. As you sit, look at these objects and allow them to lead your attention to God.

Specify concrete objects in your home or office or place of work which can remind you of particular people, needful situations, events about which you should pray.

> Teach me, my God and King
> In all things thee to see;
> And what I do in anything,
> To do it as for thee.
> —George Herbert

Symbols

O God,
 you are our constant companion. Help us to see you
 in all things.

May every object and event direct my attention
 to you.
May I find guideposts in my ordinary day
 which point to you.
May common things of life become media
 of your presence.

Give us:
 eyes to see,
 ears to hear,
 fingers to touch,
 smells and taste
 of your presence.

May daily rounds of life present
 reminders of your presence,
 incitements to prayer for others,
 and openings for service.

In the name of our incarnate Lord. Amen.

8. *Alone*

> Concerning the fittest place for heavenly meditation it is sufficient to say that the most convenient is some private retirement.... I advise that thou withdraw thyself from all society, yea, though it were a society of godly men, that thou mayst awhile enjoy the society of Christ.
> —From *The Saints' Everlasting Rest*
> by Richard Baxter

Certain moments in every day regulate the whole day.

This is the importance of setting a time each day to be alone with God. Time with God is a hinge on which other activities swing.

The chief end of a time apart is to worship God, to attend undistractedly to God's presence. It is also a time to share with God the range of neighbor concern and to seek God's will in human affairs.

A time with God revitalizes our spirit and allows the Holy Spirit to sweep through us, to engage us in communion, to set us for service. Time apart creates space for God. It cuts into the day with a new dimension and sets our life into the context of God's gracious presence.

Space for God is human privilege; it is also human necessity.

We create time and room for God by intentionally and systematically establishing a time for meditation, communion, and renewal of a sense of God's presence.

In the rhythms of life we experience engagement and detachment. There is time for activity in the world and time for quiet waiting with God. A tension must be maintained; neither aspect should be allowed to deny the other. Balanced living is most difficult to achieve, but it is also most fulfilling for Christian wholeness.

A short time ago a young mother stopped by my home to talk. After we had talked in general, she turned to me with tears in her eyes and asked, "Is it right to keep some time for one's self?" She had two children, a busy husband, and lived with many constant demands. She also wanted time alone, but when she took it she had a sense of guilt. She was afraid that to take time for herself was selfish. But I insisted that she should take time to be alone. She needed time apart, and her relation to her family and others required it. We all need both involvement and quiet retreat, and we must keep these different needs in balance with one another.

With some regularity we need "out." Away from everyone—maybe especially from those we love most—in order to get things into correct proportion again.

> Tho in the midst of others
> A part of me
> Can quietly retreat
> To privacy
> For help sufficient
> To our needs
> —Ann Marie Langford

Thomas Mann reminds us in "Death in Venice" of the double possibility of being alone. "Solitude gives birth to the original in us, to beauty unfamiliar and perilous—to poetry. But also, it gives birth to the opposite: to the perverse, the illicit, the absurd." But we must chance the misuse in order to experience the constructive and creative use of time alone. And the redeeming reality is that the time alone is not isolation. Christian solitude is never solitariness, it is always intimate, direct, involving community. Time alone is time with God.

Lawi Imathieu, from Kenya, tells how a chicken is sometimes distributed at a meal. One person after another is given his or her choice. All the good pieces go first, then only wings are left; wings—mostly bones, little meat. We treat God that way, Lawi says. We give God only the "bony" time, that which is left over.

> Good, meaty time, is needed for relationship with God.

In Isaiah 44 there is the story of an idol maker. The wood carver goes into the woods to find appropriate material from which to make his idols. He finds a tree, takes part of it to build a fire, and then cooks his food. When he is warm and full he takes, Isaiah says, "the residue" of the wood and carves an idol. Idols are made from the residue, the leftovers of life. The comment is not only about ancient idol makers but also about us. God asks us for our best. Our time with God should be good time, meaty time.

The use of special time may be as varied as a vital relationship demands. Relations constantly change; what is shared and how it is shared must always be freshly discovered. For a prayer life to grow and maintain its challenge and reward, there must be an openness to new possibility, a search for enriching interaction, deliberate exploration of new sharing.

Time apart is especially important for maturation and

new discovery in prayer. It is a time for hymns, for journal-keeping, for writing prayers, for reading, for self-examination, for simple praise, for thanksgiving, for sharing concerns. The list is as endless as creative relationship.

Time apart also creates a space for ourselves. This is not a selfish act, nor is it splendid isolation. Rather, it is a time for gathering strength, a time for personal renewal and personal growth, a time for centering, for quiet reclaiming and unforced attention on God.

Time alone with God enhances the relationship of love. Love is its own reward. Love is complete in itself for it is the fullest sharing of life with God. We love because God first loved us (1 John 4:10), and we find meaning in life in receiving and giving love in the quiet time. Love, Henry Scougal says in *The Life of God in the Soul of Man*, "is indeed the only thing we can call our own. Other things may be taken from us by violence, but none can ravish our love."

Being alone with God prepares us for going back into the whirligig of life. But time alone is not simply for the purpose of returning. We should appreciate and enjoy the value of time itself. One will return to other things. The time of gathering brings to us gifts we can share. But if the return becomes the central concern, the time apart loses its significance.

Samuel Taylor Coleridge in his *Aids to Reflection* writes,

> It is the advice of the wise man, "Dwell at home, or with yourself; and though there are very few that do this yet it is surprising that the greatest part of mankind cannot be prevailed upon, at least to visit themselves sometimes; but, according to the saying of the wise Solomon, *The eyes of the fool are in the ends of the earth.*"

In the early days of the Peace Corps training, each trainee was required to spend forty-eight hours alone. No one could take a radio or be with anyone else. If one could play a musical instrument, that could be taken. Most of the trainees found the time alone extremely difficult, and many could not stay the entire time. The requirement to be alone was simply too much for many of the young people. Only relaxation about ourselves and about the primary relation of life makes time alone a rich and nurturing experience.

With the spirit of Charles Wesley, we place ourselves at the center where peace is found. Remembering that God is the

> ... hidden source of calm repose,
> The all-sufficient love divine.

Discovery

Find:
>A quiet time.
>A quiet place.
>A quiet heart.

In self-examination, be specific. Nebulous goodness is not concrete enough. Nebulous prayers that we may "be good" are too indefinite to be helpful. Examine the situation, your self, your relationships—directly, honestly, sensitively. Pray specifically. Ask God's grace to enact the qualities of life which reflect the spirit of Jesus Christ.

> They who wait for the Lord
>   shall renew their strength,
> they shall mount up
>   with wings like eagles,
> they shall run and not be weary,
>   they shall walk and not faint.
>   —Isaiah 40:31

Read the Bible devotionally. When you use the Bible as a means of relating to God, it is better not to set a specific goal for reading, such as a chapter a day or a book a week. Rather, read in an open, expectant mood. Let the text speak to you. Read until you feel you should pause and meditate and appropriate the meaning of the scriptural word.

The greatest deterrent to prayer is inability to concentrate. We are so easily distracted. The use of mental images can be helpful in fastening one's attention. One may, as Ignatius Loyola suggested, work through the life of Christ, visualizing episodes, placing oneself in the setting, and newly discovering the meaning of faith, love, and discipleship.

Alone 63

> Bring my attention
> to rest steadily upon thee.
> Bring my affection
> to firm resolve.
> Bring my affirmation
> to constant loyalty.

A suggestion for praying in this way is to sit and relax. Imagine yourself kneeling at the altar of a familiar church. See Jesus standing before you. Then see yourself as you place in the hands of Jesus your family, your church, a globe of the world, a sick friend, a hungry child, an entire community or nation. As you offer these persons and situations to Jesus, you are releasing them into his care and invoking God's will for their lives and for your service.

"Behold, I stand at the door and knock; if anyone hears my voice and opens the door, I will come in to him and eat with him and he with me."
—Revelation 3:20

> In the castle of my soul
> Is a little postern gate,
> Whereat, when I enter,
> I am in the presence of God.
> In a moment, in the turning of a thought,
> I am where God is,
> This is a fact.
> —Walter Rauschenbusch

Prepare a spiritual journal or a prayer notebook. Copy verses, sentences, and comments which invoke the presence of God. Put down the names of persons and conditions for which you want to pray. Write out some of your prayers. Write your reflections on particular words such as *love*, or *kindness*, or *faithfulness*.

Let my heart
The piercing wound of thy swift love receive.
—From *An Anthology of the Love of God*
   by Evelyn Underhill

Leave it all quietly to God, my soul,
   my rescue comes from him alone;
rock, rescue, refuge, he is all to me,
   never shall I be overthrown.
—Psalm 62:1 (Moffatt)

Thou hidden source of calm repose,
Thou all-sufficient love divine,
My help and refuge from my foes,
Secure I am if thou art mine;
And lo! from sin and grief and shame,
I hide me, Jesus, in thy name.
—Charles Wesley

At the heart of the cyclone tearing the sky
And flinging the clouds and the towers by
   Is a place of central calm:
So here in the roar of mortal things,
I have a place where my spirit sings,
   In the hollow of God's Palm.
—Edwin Markham

Time Alone

O Lord, help me to see and understand myself properly in relation to other people. I set myself in your will and seek to find myself as your child. Melt me, mold me, fill me with your gracious love.

Let me relax into your keeping. Remove anxiety, renew me by your love. For these few minutes, let me not rush, or press for results, or talk too much. Help me to trust your sovereign goodness, to breathe deeply of your spirit. It is good to spend time with you, to rest in your sustaining presence.

As I think and read and pray, may I do it in the quiet confidence that my life rests in you.

In the spirit and name of Jesus. Amen.

9. Friends

Life is created to be shared. Persons are created for covenant relation with God, and God created persons for relationships in community with other persons. Human life, therefore, finds significance as it is shared with God and with other people. Our lives deepen through interaction with others.

We experience the value of community in every event of life, such as eating, entertainment, work, or service. I once went to study in England. I was alone and had much library work to do. I found that I tended to eat more quickly and with less interest because eating is more of a social, sharing event than I had realized. To break the monotony, I went to some movies and then realized how sharing with others enriches even watching a movie.

In every area of life the value of community is basic. And so it is in spiritual experience.

Finding a spiritual friend or friends is important. We need to explore possibilities but not enforce stereotypes in searching for such relationships.

Growth as an individual is set within the context of community. Personal spiritual growth is enhanced by friendship which is honest, provocative, and encouraging.

"It is grace," Dietrich Bonhoeffer exclaims in *Life Together*, "nothing but grace, that we are allowed to live in community with Christian brethren."

We need to see ourselves as others see us. We need our judgments checked by others who care more about our reality than they do about our opinions about our reality. We need to be able to share our joy and sorrow, to test our understanding, to interpret scripture with others, to pray together. It is a grace of God to give us a spiritual companion or companions to walk with us along the "way."

Spiritual friendship may be found in intimate one-on-one interaction or in small, intimate groups. The value of small groups, spiritual counselors and religious communities, and neighborhood prayer groups, have been found important. But too often we have not availed ourselves of intentional spiritual communities.

Spiritual community is one of the means of spiritual maturing. A person can only go so far—and that a rather short distance—alone.

It is a part of communion with God to sustain lively communion with other persons. Yet it is difficult to share time in a full way. We are distracted, always re-doing the past and re-planning the future, replaying the game, rehearsing a conversation, redoing the task—and almost always at the expense of our present company and activity. Family and friends are usually the ones whom we neglect even when we are nominally present. We assume that they will continue to be there.

The significant present is created by God's significant presence.

Normal, spontaneous human relationships may be a sign of the awareness of God's presence and an evidence of our true presence with others. Listening and speaking are both necessary. To hear what another is saying is evidence of our respect for his or her presence and for communication with us. To speak directly with another and to listen attentively indicates the seriousness and joy with which we take his or her contribution to our lives. Every relationship needs to be set within God's presence. The present time is good. God has given it to us, and we should affirm its goodness.

Affirm the present! Such affirmation is a necessity of meaningful living with other persons. When I was in the first grade, my teacher taught us the following poem.

> Look not for fresher founts afar,
> Just drop your bucket where you are.

In terms of relationships that is good advice. Take the moment given, and turn full attention to the one or ones with you.

We have a need and privilege, when sharing with a friend or friends, not to concentrate upon our inner life alone, not to spend time in unnecessary introspection or spiritual self-culture. On the contrary, such time will become more important as—together—we share concern about the world, about human conditions, about specific persons, political situations, economic deprivation, peace, social injustice. To pray together is not to offer prayers only for one another, but may also evoke an enrichment of general sensitivity and shared concern for larger issues in the world.

> *Prayer always leads beyond self to God and the neighbor. Spiritual friendships are important as they reinforce us in the larger awareness.*

Solitary religion tends to be moribund. Shared life is a special gift of God, and we need to find concrete ways of sharing.

Discovery

> He bids us build each other up;
> And, gathered into one,
> To our high calling's glorious hope,
> We hand in hand go on.
> —Charles Wesley

> "Where two or three are gathered in my name, there am I in the midst of them."
> —Matthew 18:20

Thus the real life of that Church consists in the mutual love and dependence, the common prayer, adoration and self-offering of the whole inter-penetrating family of spirits who have dared to open their souls without condition to the all-demanding, all-giving Spirit of Charity, in Whom we live and move and without Whom we should not exist.
—From *An Anthology of the Love of God* by Evelyn Underhill

For some people it may be of value to seek a group or a friend with whom you can share your spiritual interests. Make time to study, pray, and serve together. Begin with modest expectations. Attempt what you can realistically do. Let the relationship and the responsibilities grow in their own way. Artificial community is of no value. Sharing should be simple and sincere.

Dietrich Bonhoeffer writes in *Life Together*,

> "Behold, how good and how pleasant it is for brethren to dwell together in unity"—this is the Scripture's praise of life together under the Word. But now we can rightly interpret the words "in unity" and say, "for brethren to dwell together *through Christ*." For Jesus Christ alone is our unity. "He is our peace." Through him alone do we have access to one another, joy in one another, and fellowship with one another.

Friends

Most gracious God,
  Our lives are enriched by other lives.
  We receive our lives from you and we grow
    as our communion with you grows.
  We also receive life from other persons and we
    grow through friendship and sharing.
  Enrich us in every meeting, in every shared moment.

Help us to give love freely and to accept love gladly.
  May we seek out and live within meaningful relationships. Where friendship is lacking, lead us to new opportunity and new experience of life together with other people.

Good relationship is one of your choice gifts.
  May our lives be enriched by those human relationships you intend for us. Lead the right persons into our lives, make us receptive and responsive to them. Lead us to those others whom we can enrich by our friendship.

  In the name of our companion, Jesus Christ. Amen.

10. *Family*

Family relationships are a part of shared time, but, because of their importance, we lift them up for special attention. The family is the basic human community through which persons are nurtured and sustained in mutual love and responsibility. *Family* is not simply defined. Groupings into family are as diverse as human community. A family may be a married couple, a parent and children, or several generations living together. No two families are alike and no family remains the same over time. But whatever the particular arrangements, people together as a family are the primary community in which daily spiritual nurture takes place. Development takes place in the family, whether for good or bad.

God has given families to enrich and test, to renew and stretch, to guide and thwart family members. The place of highest joy may also be the place of deepest pain; the place of fulfillment may also be the place of frustration. Family relationships provide the most immediate arena for experiencing distress and grace.

There is remarkable endurance about family ties. One may at times feel that, as Robert Frost says in "The Death of the Hired Man":

> Home is the place where, when you have to go there,
> They have to take you in.

But families often give more than necessary reception. How often when wills are drawn the executor is a family member. And this is so even if there are closer friends or if the family member is distant in geography and shared life. A bond continues because there is a family tie.

But family life is not always positive. We are learning, often to our astonishment, how widespread is child abuse or sexual harrassment within families. Even more prevalent are psychological attacks and radical oscillation between love and hate. G. K. Chesterton in "The House of Christmas" speaks of a common human condition:

> For men are homesick in their homes,
> And strangers under the sun,
> And they lay their heads in a foreign land
> Whenever the day is done.

We do not need to idealize or deny the importance of the family. Realism is necessary. Over idealization brings guilt and sense of failure; denial often destroys the possibility which actually exists. Because families are our most immediate and influential communities, they express the best and the worst, as well as of the joy and ordinariness of our existence.

Because families are so important, it is fundamental that there be a spiritual dimension in family life.

Families are a primary arena in which Christian faith is embodied and Christian character (or lack of it) is most clearly evident.

Love realized through marriage is a triune experience. We are held together by God's encompassing arms. So joy and pain are shared together and with God. So human relationships endure because of divine forgiveness and renewal—which invoke our forgiveness and renewal. Human love finds its depth and its outreach in God's love. The truest human relationships are relationships "in God."

Prayer and the common life must consider the family

and its spiritual character. Nothing is more helpful or more difficult than meaningful family prayer.

Many old traditions have disappeared, and few families now pray together on a regular basis. A number of practical realities militate against family time together: different schedules, different rhythms of daily activity, varying time of emotional readiness, and lack of significant materials to guide thought and prayer are among the most obvious. Yet, in spite of these difficulties which conspire to make time together unfruitful for shared activity, it is within our families that prayer life should be discovered or enriched.

To be homeless is to be rootless. This fact makes it necessary not only to build up the positive factors in our own home but also to be concerned for all homeless persons: those who live alone, those who have lost homes through death of a family member, or as runaway adolescents, mentally ill or abandoned persons, those who are house-bound, or are unable to establish a home.

The value of family is realized not only in families already established but in the creation of families which do not yet exist.

A relation exists between having a home and making a home, between homecoming and home-giving. Families are enriched not only by enjoying one another—and that is a great good—but by also sharing together in significant responsibilities, sorrows, causes, or tasks to be done.

Creation of true family meaning requires thought and effort. We need to think about the family and decide what it ought to do, share, forego, participate in, abstain from, and work for. There are constant temptations for one person to do everything for everyone, or for each to do his or her own thing in isolation from the others. Family time should allow freedom for each to have time alone, but it should also provide clear opportunity to be together.

Discovery

> Lord, let us in our homes agree
> This blessed peace to gain;
> Unite our hearts in love to thee,
> And love to all will reign.
> —Henry Ware, Jr.

> O happy home, where Thou art not forgotten
> When joy is overflowing, full, and free;
> O happy home, where every wounded spirit
> Is brought, Physician, Comforter, to Thee—
> —Carl J. P. Spitta

Make the grace before meals a special occasion. Think ahead. Be personal. Perhaps the family can join hands around the table. Let different members say the blessing. Sometimes sing. A little preparation can change routine into a holy moment.

Use the seasons of the church year. During such times as Advent and Lent make a special effort to arrange family time for shared devotions. Set aside a meal or an evening time when there can be Bible reading and prayer. Different family members can take responsibility. Use the opportunity for discussion. The length of time is not as important as its regularity, its good use, and the sense of the importance of shared devotion.

As your family changes, rethink the ways you can be together. Make prayer for one another a regular habit. Find times when you can all share in recreation. How can you make holidays more meaningful? How can members give one another needed support? Also look for opportunities for the family to share in mission such as world hunger, family financial gifts, projects of service done together. Let there be full and free discussion of Christian faith and its relation to service.

Family

We thank you, O Lord God, for our families, for life bound together, for love to give and to receive, for care and readiness to respond, for common responsibilities and joy.

I pray for each member of my family. May we all keep growing and spiritually maturing. Hear my prayer for ____ and ____ and ____.

We pray for the larger human family,
    for sensitivity to need,
    for resolution to act and speak
    from loving motives.

Hear our prayer for ____ and ____ and ____ .

We pray for our family in Christ, for life changed by your love and for shared commitment. With thanksgiving, we commend our family into your keeping.
In Jesus' name. Amen.

11. Charity

> Action and Contemplation are very close companions; they live together in one house on equal terms; Martha is Mary's sister.
> —St. Bernard of Clairvaux

Prayer does not lead so much to an emotional high as to a useful life. The test of our belief is in our practice.

Along with ordinary daily tasks, we should practice special works of love. Neighbor love requires concrete expression. The incarnation was God's identification with the human condition, and Jesus left us a commandment, "Love one another as I have loved you" (John 15:12).

Spiritual life has authenticity as it takes shape in concrete helpfulness to other persons. Hence, the natural and necessary development of true spirituality finds outlet where there is specific need.

The agenda of every Christian life must include time for serving activity.

The proper relation between prayer and service is not that service is supremely important and prayer may help it, but that prayer is supremely important and conduct tests it. Yet these two are inseparable: genuine prayer always issues in faithful service; moral action is a branch growing from the vigorous root of religious commitment.

Wolfram von Eschenbach, in commenting on the character of Sigune in Wagner's opera *Parsival*, says, "her whole life was a kneeling." Such kneeling may have a double significance, as prayer and as service. To be alive to Christ is to be aware of the world and its need. To be alive to Christ is to be alive to others.

Prayer reinforces our strength and makes our hands adroit in caring for others. Our spirit is receptive in prayer, and receptivity is transposed through prayer into activity. Being with God places us in the service of other persons.

It is a part of Christian responsibility to seek those in special need and find ways we can be helpful through both personal and social structures. We should regularly give time to such service. This means that a regularly scheduled or a specifically arranged activity is a basic dimension of a Christian style of living.

The mode of this service may range widely. It may be a personal relation to a person or family in need, such as visitation in a home or hospital; it may be political activity for some change; it may be support for community organization; it may be carrying meals on wheels, working for alleviation of world hunger; it may be a prison program or public interest matters.

There is some wisdom in finding an outlet which involves one in an unfamiliar arena of life, to move beyond the normal boundaries of our contacts and relationships. Personal growth as well as an opportunity for service may be enhanced by stretching beyond the comfortable confines of our usual rounds.

J. B. Phillips has translated Second Timothy 3:5 in a telling fashion. In speaking of deceitful persons, the author comments, "They... maintain a façade of 'religion' but their life denies its truth." So is the religious pretension that does not carry vital faith into encompassing life.

Here is another important principle of Christian discipleship:

> *Find a situation in which you can make a concrete contribution to other people.* Prayers bear fruit in human living as communion with God is carried into other relationships. Prayer makes us contributors to others.

Discipline is required to do works of charity. It takes thought, energy, and resolution to find where we can serve and to serve faithfully over time. The discipline of regular commitment means that our lives must be organized around these obligations, and our conveniences must often yield to other necessities.

Not only must we cultivate sensitive awareness of need, we must undertake specific activity to meet need. Decide how much time you should give, then look carefully to find how you want to invest this part of yourself. Make a clear commitment as to what you will do, and make this activity a part of your intercessory prayer. Give yourself faithfully to the task.

Service needs structure. If we leave ourselves to drift, to undertake tasks only with unplanned spontaneity, we nearly always drift into doing little service. We often deceive ourselves about how much service we are performing. Neighbor responsibility implies disciplined, regular, faithful activity; it is regular and regulates our efforts.

A prayer group in Massachusetts found that committing four hours a week by each person to some special cause proved a vital enrichment to the life of prayer. The cause may be one of justice. It may be research to understand problems in society and work for structural change in social order. The cause may be helping a person who has special need, resettling an immigrant family, volunteering work in a hospital, assisting in grocery buying for a person who cannot do this well, tutoring children—the possibilities are limitless. From among the possibilities, choose a definite task to which you can commit yourself, and do it regularly.

The use of money and time are both important. Prayer involves stewardship. It is self-giving as response to God's self-giving. It is a holy privilege to share in God's identification with the world.

When we move out of the center of our own lives, the chief impediment of our vision vanishes. We can begin to see God in everything. Prayer is an assault on our self-predilections and an expansion of horizon and responsibility.

Self-complacency is almost always a sign of spiritual stagnation. Being wrapped up in our own interests prevents our growth through interest in others.

Discovery

> Since Christ embraced the Crosse itselfe, dare I
> His image, th' image of his Crosse deny?
> Would I have profit by the sacrifice,
> And dare the chosen altar to despise?
> It bore all other sinnes, but is it fit
> That it should beare the sinne of scorning it?
> —From "The Cross" by John Donne

O God, you are the source of all life, its goodness and beauty, its joy and sensitivity. Make me aware of the fullness of thy presence, and may I share this fullness with others. Sensitize me to rejoice with those who rejoice and to weep with those who weep. Align my life with those in special need: the poor and oppressed, the spiritually and economically deprived, the lonely and hurt, the hungry and lost. Give to me today the tasks you have for me to do as expressions of your love. In the name of Jesus who identified with our condition and need. Amen.

> Give us, O God, the strength to build
> The city that hath stood
> Too long a dream, whose laws are love,
> Whose ways are brotherhood,
> And where the sun that shineth is
> God's grace for human good.
> —Walter Russell Bowie

We pray for:

> All who love and serve your city,
> all who bear its daily stress,
> all who cry for peace and justice,
> all who curse and all who bless.
> —Erik Routley

Frederik Herman Kaan has based a verse on Luke 1:46-55.

> He calls us to revolt and fight
> with him for what is just and right,
> to sing and live Magnificat
> in crowded street and walkup flat.

Find a concrete project to which you can contribute. Look around your community for a place of special need or a cause which you can serve. For instance, the alleviation of hunger may be your special calling. Decide how you can invest several hours a week in this responsibility. Determine a plan and be faithful.

What are other possibilities? Visitation, political issues, a nursing home, volunteer work? "Let each of you look not only to his own interests, but also to the interest of others" (Phil. 2:4).

Toyohiko Kagawa, a Japanese Christian who worked in the slums of Kobe, had a vision.

> My eyes behold Thee here,
> And when I close them
> I
> Can feel Thee watching
> By my side.
>
> Farewell to paper-pasted walls;
> I get me up
> And shove my shoddy sandals on.
>
> Throughout this land
> I go to preach,
> *"The Kingdom is at hand!"*
> —From *Songs from the Slums*

Charity

O Lord, carry our prayers into active engagement with life. May our prayers make us more sensitive to the negative and limiting conditions of life, more ready to challenge injustice and misuse of power. Make our understanding of wrong conditions clearer. Make us firmer in our opposition to evil, more willing to give, to risk, and to serve.

Give to us the special tasks which we can do. Make us ready to accept particular responsibilities, more committed to social well-being, more repulsed by human sin, more aware of structured maladjustments of life.

Draw us through our prayers into your world. May we struggle in a prayerful spirit, offering our service, our concerns, our efforts, our lives into your providential keeping.

In the name of Jesus, who came to redeem all of human life. Amen.

12. Style

Prayer, as a centering activity of Christian living, sets our styles of life. The reality of prayer shapes the way in which we live. This principle may be put succinctly: as we pray, so we live.

The relationship with God realized in prayer is reflected in all of our relationships with fellow humans. Every encounter is influenced and shaped by the central encounter of prayer. Every action is given direction and purpose by the foundation established in prayer.

The ways in which primary relationships govern secondary relationships are obvious in the usual rounds of life. For instance, when marriage is of primary importance to us we look at a question of job location, of other relationships, or of recreation in terms of how these affect, may contribute to, or may have negative influence on our marriage. Consequently, we ask: in the light of this primary relationship, what should I decide about this or that possibility?

If one's life is not in conformity with one's professed beliefs, spiritual disaster occurs; there is a terrible tearing of wholeness, a disruption of existence which always ends in deterioration of both belief and life. Not to be shaped by one's professed beliefs is the same as to acknowledge that one does not truly believe what one professes. Life is styled by faith. Gottfried von Strassburg, the medieval German poet, in his *Tristan and Isold* speaks of Isold, "Her life took shape as the very image of the need so close to her heart."

Two factors—simplicity and community—stand out when we meet God in prayer. First, prayer centers life upon God. That center gives shape to every aspect of life. We put away excess interests and activity.

We find maturation in Christian living as we center more and more of life upon God.

The potentialities we possess are multiple. Every human being has ability to move in many different directions, to use his or her talents for a large variety of ends, to care about many things, and to seek multiple goods. This capacity may lead to idolatry—that is, to substituting a lesser good for the greatest good. But, when drawn by God's love, our abilities and talents find focus in the love of God; and that love gives order to all of life.

To live simply is to have our priorities straight. It is to make each decision in the light of our primary decisions; it is to live for God as the first and most important reality.

Simple living is life lived with the keen awareness of God as our sacred center.

Simple love of God implies a simplification of the rest of our lives. We should concentrate more on what is genuinely needed than on what we want. Simplicity carries a rejection of wastefulness. It implies good stewardship, a willingness to give our abundance to God and not to use it in self-centered ways.

Such simplicity governs all our lives: the clothes we wear, the food we eat, the use of our money, the expenditure of our time. To pray sincerely sets the center and the circumference of our living.

Currently we hear that small is beautiful, that less can be more, that restriction may lead to fullness. In Christian living this is the case. Sharp focus on God arranges the pattern of our living, and it is a pattern cut to the material of our lives in wise and responsible ways.

Prayer simplifies our lives. It keeps the center clear and boundaries are held by that center.

John Fowles, the English novelist, has also written a short history of Stonehenge, *The Enigma of Stonehenge*. In his discussion of the awesome simplicity of that stone monument, he asks why the search for mysticism is so often found in our own gadget-filled society. He asked a woman from California about this and her answer was "too much". We have too much of so many things that we clutter our lives with trivial, petty, insignificant "gadgets". Simplicity retains impressive dignity and it adds clarity to life.

Thomas Kelly has spoken to these matters as clearly and helpfully as any recent writer. In *A Testament of Devotion* he affirms that "Life is meant to be lived from a Center, a divine Center." It is the integrating power of this center which draws the complexity of our lives into a coherent and meaningful pattern. Yet, complexity remains. Consequently, Kelly adds practical advice.

But we must not spend precious time merely stating the problem. And although we all enjoy feeling sorry for ourselves, we must not linger long, bewailing the poverty of life induced by the overabundance of our opportunities. Nor must we rush hastily at a solution, breathlessly anxious for once to get something, this day, to show for the time we've spent upon our problem. Prune and trim we must, but not with ruthless haste and ready pruning knife, until we have reflected upon the tree we trim, the environment it lives in, and the sap of life which feeds it.

The advice is wise. Simplification of life is important, indeed one of the most necessary actions in an age of affluence. But simplification requires wisdom. We should thoughtfully decide how our love of God should structure our economic life, our buying decisions, our giving of gifts, the style and quality of our homes and cars, our contributions to world hunger, to economic deprivation, or our acceptance of responsibilities, the use of our time, and the offer of our affections.

> *Simplification is a process, an ongoing integration of more and more of life around its sacred center.*

To live a simplified life is to be able to give clearer answers to the claims upon our lives. It is to be able to say yes with a hearty sense of goodness, and to say no with a relaxed sense of rightness.

In the second place, prayer binds our lives with all human life. To pray to God, "Our Father..." is to learn immediately that the love of God carries, inevitably, to the love of our neighbor.

> *An early discovery in the life of prayer is that we never come to God alone.*

Often the question is asked, why should we pray for others? Doesn't God already know their need? (Certainly.) Isn't God more concerned for every person than we can possibly be for any person? (Certainly.) Aren't we liable to attempt to mold the other person in the image we (rather than God) have for them? (Possibly.) Does God refuse to act for others' well being until we pray? (Certainly not.) Is there some lack in God's good will that our prayer fulfills? (Certainly not.) Then why pray for others?

The question is put in terms of necessity. But it should be put in terms of privilege: how can a Christian not pray for others? Is it not a character of Christian life that we carry a love and concern for others as fundamental to our way of living? So we pray for others as a natural expression of our love of God. It is our privilege to share others with God in love.

Prayers of intercession are the spontaneous and disciplined means of expressing the binding of life in Christ.

Prayers of intercession are a concrete expression of life lived in awareness of others, of their needs and our abilities to aid. Prayer is always a partial expression of what is true in the wholeness of life. And the whole life, in God, always includes life with and for others.

There are two aspects of prayerful living—simplicity and community—and these are controlling in our developing style of living. Christian style is a maturing way of life. It is the result of attentive discipline, as is the style of a writer, a painter, a musician. It does not come full blown and complete. Rather it is developed by hard work; it is an expression of one's values and purposes.

We shall learn to appreciate persons who have "real style." There is no pretension in this style. It is not a matter of sheen and show. This style is not mere stylishness, a mimicry of the latest fad. Rather, it is a style of mature graciousness, an ability to move among people with empathy and love.

Christian style exhibits a willingness to be spent, a quickness to serve, and a commitment to the cause of the good. Convincing style has been expressed in radically different personalities: an exuberant Francis of Assisi, a restless John Wesley, a many-talented Albert Schweitzer. It may also be expressed in a faithful carpenter, a diligent business executive, a local pastor, a dedicated teacher, a cheerful salesperson.

Christian faith can never be parochial. It cannot carve out little enclaves for comfortable living. Jesus Christ reorients and then reorganizes our living. A new center brings with it a new style of living.

The Quakers have a quaint question which, nevertheless, touches our present life. "Has truth been advancing among you?" they ask. By this they mean, is there growth? Is there the movement of life toward God? Is life being continuously formed by grace?

By lively relationship with Christ, the normal and regular and common things of life are set within a new arena and they are undertaken in a new spirit. The gospel of grace is embodied in our ways of living.

Discovery

> As each far horizon beckons,
>   may it challenge us anew,
> children of creative purpose,
>   serving others, honoring you.
> May our dreams prove rich with promise,
>   each endeavor well begun:
> Great Creator, give us guidance
>   till our goals and yours are one.
>   —Catherine Cameron

> In the maelstrom of the nations,
> in the journeying into space,
> in the clash of generations
> in the hungering for grace,
> in our agony and glory,
> we are called to newer ways
> by the Lord of our tomorrows
> and the God of earth's today.
>   —T. Herbert O'Driscoll

Our style of life reflects our values. Take time to assess your values. Write them down. Discuss them with family or a friend. Decide how your life can better reflect these values. Be specific, set goals.

Review your attitudes toward money. How do your spending habits reflect your values? How do they not?

How may your life be simplified and made more useful in serving others? What things are most needful for you? What is excess?

> I say more: the just man justices;
> Keeps grace: that keeps all his goings graces;
> Acts in God's eye what in God's eye he is—
> Christ. For Christ plays in ten thousand places,
> Lovely in limbs, and lovely in eyes not his
> To the Father through the features of men's faces.
>   —From "As Kingfishers Catch Fire"
>   by Gerard Manley Hopkins

> So, whether you eat or drink, or whatever you do, do all to the glory of God.
> —1 Corinthians 10:31

> Lay me on an anvil, O God.
> Beat me and hammer me into a crowbar.
> Let me pry loose old walls.
> Let me lift and loosen old foundations.
> —From "Prayers of Steel" by Carl Sandburg

Style

O Lord, draw my life into conformity with your will. Help me to remember and respond to Jesus' word, "A new commandment I give to you, that you love one another; even as I have loved you, that you will also love one another" (John 13:34).

Bring my life into sharply focused love. Integrate my living around its true center. May every expression of my life be a reflection of your grace and goodness.

Give "style" to my life, the style of Jesus Christ who came as a servant, who happily gave himself, who lived humbly, recreatively, faithfully, challengingly.

Simplify my wants.
Enrich my sense of community.
Make me participant in the lives of those in need.
Give me sensitive awareness and tenacious
 strength to do what is right.

Form me by your will; order my living. Give clear purpose to my life.

In the name of him in whose image we seek to grow. Amen.

13. Close of Day

The ending of a day, the completing of another time of activity, tiredness, the coming of darkness and preparation for sleep—all these factors bring remembrance, reflection, repentance, and a need to trust and hope.

Night! The end of day time anticipates the final time. Darkness is a foreshadowing of death and last things, a movement into the unknown. Night closes off horizons and we approach the dark with tremors. Bill Cosby tells a story of his childhood experience of darkness. His mother would stop by his bed and say, "Now don't be afraid, nothing will get you." And, of course, it reminded him that something might get him. He would see a shadow and would pull his covers over his head. As long as he was under the covers nothing, he believed, would get him. But he had to come up for air. So he would, as quickly as he could, pull back the covers, draw a breath, then jerk the covers over his head again. The darkness often carries a sense of impending trouble.

Facing the night, we are aware of the cessation of power to govern our lives, of our inability to control our destinies. We are in the hands of God. No other resource remains, no human strength is adequate; we must now close our eyes and release our lives. Approach to these mysteries can bring either fear or relaxed confidence.

> *The close of every day is a token indication of the final closure of mortal existence. We are thrown upon ultimate ends and into the keeping of the Ultimate.*

The end of the day may bring fulfillment or despair, a sense of failure or faithfulness, and often a mixture of both. In the dark, our past is recalled, and we glance into the shadowed expanse of the future.

Here the Christian message speaks to us. For the end of the day, which can bring despair and a sense of uncertainty, may also bring a sense of relaxation into the keeping of God.

People are, at times, embarrassed that they go to sleep saying their prayers. This can be embarrassing, because one wants to be attentive, thoughtful, able to complete the prayer. And this may be a sign of indifference. But this may also be a sign of grace and trust. Overarching and underlying our living is the sovereign presence of God. We go to sleep in God.

But insomnia is also a reality. So much comes before us: good memories, joy, a meaningful word, a happy encounter, service done; and also disappointments, failures, angry words, insensitivity, even denial or forgetfulness of God. Thanksgiving and penance are both spontaneous and appropriate responses. Our day runs quickly through our awareness. When we come to the close of the day and face the haunt of uncertainty and threatening powers, we may experience fear. But this may also be a special time when God is with us.

> Good memories are brought forth:
> tiredness from work well done
> recreation enjoyed
> relationships fulfilled
> service rendered
> a sense of divine presence.
>
> Thanksgiving spontaneously wells-up.

> Disappointments are revived:
>   things done or said
>   activities
>   relationships abused
>   insensitivity
>   lack of courage
>   denial of God.

Samuel Taylor Coleridge reminds us in *Aids to Reflection* of a dark tendency. "There is an aching hollowness in the bosom, a dark cold speck at the heart, an obscure and boding sense of a somewhat, that must be kept out of sight of the conscience; some secret lodger, whom they can neither resolve to eject or retain." The point is: bring everything out! Present your total life to God. And know that God forgives, and makes new; God sets aside and sets right.

> Though your sins are like scarlet,
>   they shall be as white as snow;
> though they are red like crimson,
>   they shall become like wool.
>   —Isaiah 1:18

Penance is necessary, forgiveness is asked... and, in Christ, it is given.

Darkness may be a haunt of terrors, a fear of being alone, a sense of threatening powers; or it may be a time of relaxed confidence in God's good presence which is with us in this and every night.

A minister visited a sick parishioner. She asked him to pray. He did. Then he asked her to pray. She prayed, "Now I lay me down to sleep..." It was the only prayer she had ever uttered. But, he said, she really prayed those words.

Discovery

> From the rising of the sun to its setting
> the name of the Lord is to be praised!
> —Psalm 113:3

One of the losses accompanying the cessation of Sunday evening services has been the loss of opportunity to sing vesper hymns. Some of the most beautiful hymns in Christendom are those which accompany the close of day. To re-pray some of these hymns can give expression to trusting faith.

> Softly now the light of day
> Fades upon our sight away;
> Free from care, from labor free,
> Lord, we would commune with thee.
> —George W. Doane

> Now the day is over,
> Night is drawing nigh;
> Shadows of the evening
> Steal across the sky.
> Jesus, give the weary
> Calm and sweet repose;
> With thy tenderest blessing
> May our eyelids close.
> —Sabine Baring-Gould

> Savior, breathe an evening blessing,
> Ere repose our spirits seal;
> Sin and want we come confessing;
> Thou canst save, and thou canst heal.
> —John Edmeston

> Thine is the day, thine also the night.
> —Psalm 74:16

> The day thou gavest, Lord, is ended,
> The darkness falls at thy behest;
> To thee our morning hymns ascended,
> Thy praise shall sanctify our rest.
> —John Ellerton

A way of praying is to visualize in your mind's eye a series of acts as you enter a room. 1) Close the door. Turn away from all other issues and activities. 2) Take off your hat. Recognize that you are in the presence of the Divine and be reverent. 3) Open the window. Allow the fresh Spirit of God to blow into your life. 4) Sit down. Relax in the presence of God. Allow the time to develop its own meaning.*

> In peace I will both lie down and sleep;
> for thou alone, O Lord, makest me dwell in safety.
> —Psalm 4:8

> I heard the voice of Jesus say,
> "Come unto me and rest;
> Lay down, thou weary one, lay down
> Thy head upon my breast."
> I came to Jesus as I was,
> Weary and worn and sad;
> I found in him a resting place,
> And he has made me glad.
> —Horatius Bonar

---

*This procedure is loosely based on *An Autobiography of Prayer* by Albert Edward Day (New York: Harper & Brothers, 1952), pp. 103-4.

Close of Day

At the close of this day, O Lord,
    we commend our lives
        into thy keeping.
Thou art our creator,
    our sustainer,
    our everlasting hope.
In the care of thy love,
    we lie down in trust
        and rest.

In Jesus' name. Amen.